DOMAIN-SPECIFIC LANGUAGES MASTERY

THE POWER OF CUSTOM LANGUAGE

OLIVER LUCAS JR

Copyright © 2024 by Oliver Lucas Jr

All rights reserved. No part of this publication may be reproduced, distributed, or transmitted in any form or by any means, including photocopying, recording, or other electronic or mechanical methods, without the prior written permission of the publisher, except in the case of brief quotations embodied in critical reviews and certain other non commercial uses permitted by copyright law.

TABLE OF CONTENTS

Chapter 1

1.1 Why DSLs Matter
1.2 Types of DSLs (Internal vs. External)
1.3 Benefits and Challenges

Chapter 2

2.1 Abstract Syntax Trees (ASTs
2.2 Grammars and Parsing
2.3 Semantic Analysis

Chapter 3

3.1 Understanding Your Domain
3.2 Data Processing and Analysis (SQL, R)
3.3 Prioritizing Usability

Chapter 4

4.1 Leveraging Host Language Features
4.2 API Design for DSLs
4.3 Examples in Popular Languages (Java, Python, etc.)

Chapter 5

5.1 Lexical Analysis and Parsing Techniques
5.2 Building Interpreters and Compilers
5.3 Code Generation Strategies

Chapter 6

6.1 Metaprogramming and Macros
6.2 Domain-Specific Modeling (DSM)

6.3 Testing and Debugging DSLs

Chapter 7

7.1 Web Development (HTML, CSS)
7.2 Data Processing and Analysis (SQL, R)
7.3 DevOps and Infrastructure Automation

Chapter 8

8.1 Code Generation and Automation
8.2 Reducing Boilerplate Code
8.3 Improving Code Readability and Maintainability

Chapter 9

9.1 Successful DSL Implementations
9.2 Lessons Learned and Best Practices
9.3 Analyzing DSL Design Choices

Chapter 10

10.1 Analyzing DSL Design Choices
10.2 Cloud-Based DSL Development
10.3 The Future of Language Engineering

Preface

In the ever-evolving landscape of software development, where complexity reigns and efficiency is paramount, Domain-Specific Languages (DSLs) have emerged as a powerful tool for taming the chaos and empowering developers to express solutions with elegance and precision. This book, "Domain-Specific Languages Mastery: The Power of Custom Languages," is your guide to unlocking the potential of DSLs and harnessing their transformative capabilities.

Whether you're a seasoned software engineer seeking to optimize your workflows or a curious developer eager to explore new frontiers in language design, this book will equip you with the knowledge and skills to create DSLs that streamline development, enhance communication, and elevate your software to new heights.

Within these pages, we embark on a journey through the fascinating world of DSLs, delving into their diverse types, their underlying principles, and their myriad applications. We'll explore the art of designing DSLs that seamlessly integrate with your domain, crafting syntax and semantics that capture the essence of your problem space. We'll uncover the techniques for implementing DSLs, from leveraging the power of host languages to constructing parsers and interpreters that breathe life into your custom creations.

But this book is more than just a technical manual. It's an invitation to embrace a new way of thinking about software development, one that prioritizes clarity, conciseness, and collaboration. We'll delve into real-world case studies, drawing inspiration from successful DSL implementations and gleaning valuable lessons from past experiences. We'll explore the future of DSLs, examining their role in emerging technologies like artificial intelligence and cloud computing.

As you embark on this journey, remember that DSLs are not merely about code; they're about empowering developers and domain experts to communicate effectively, to express solutions with clarity, and to build software that is both powerful and elegant. With this book as your guide, you'll discover the transformative power of DSLs and unlock a new realm of possibilities in your software development endeavors.

Join us as we delve into the world of DSLs and discover the power of custom languages to transform your software and elevate your craft.

Chapter 1

Introduction to DSLs

1.1 Why DSLs Matter

1. Increased Productivity and Efficiency:

Reduced Boilerplate: DSLs allow developers to express complex logic with less code, eliminating repetitive tasks and reducing errors.

Faster Development: By focusing on the domain's essential concepts, DSLs streamline development, allowing for quicker iterations and faster time-to-market.

Improved Maintainability: Concise and readable DSL code is easier to understand and maintain, reducing the cost of long-term software evolution.

2. Enhanced Communication and Collaboration:

Bridging the Gap: DSLs provide a common language between domain experts and developers, facilitating better communication and understanding of requirements.

Empowering Domain Experts: DSLs enable domain experts to directly express their knowledge and participate in the software development process, leading to more accurate and relevant solutions.

Improved Collaboration: By providing a shared understanding of the domain, DSLs foster better collaboration among team members with diverse backgrounds.

3. Reduced Complexity and Errors:

Abstraction and Focus: DSLs abstract away low-level details, allowing developers to focus on the core logic of the domain, reducing cognitive load and potential errors.

Domain-Specific Validation: DSLs can incorporate domain-specific constraints and validation rules, ensuring that the code adheres to the domain's rules and preventing invalid states.

Increased Reliability: By reducing complexity and enforcing domain constraints, DSLs contribute to more reliable and robust software systems.

4. Increased Flexibility and Adaptability:

Tailored Solutions: DSLs enable the creation of highly customized solutions that precisely address the specific needs of the domain.

Easier Evolution: As the domain evolves, DSLs can be adapted to accommodate new requirements and changes, ensuring that the software remains relevant and maintainable.

Improved Reusability: DSLs can be reused across multiple projects within the same domain, promoting consistency and reducing development effort.

In essence, DSLs empower developers and domain experts to create software that is more efficient, reliable, and aligned with the specific needs of the domain. By providing a higher level of abstraction, DSLs unlock new possibilities for software development, making it more accessible, productive, and impactful.

1.2 Types of DSLs (Internal vs. External)

Internal DSLs

Embedded within a Host Language: Internal DSLs are built within an existing general-purpose programming language (like Java, Python, or Ruby). They leverage the host language's syntax and semantics, extending it to create a domain-specific vocabulary.

Fluent Interfaces and Method Chaining: Internal DSLs often use method chaining and fluent interfaces to create expressive and readable code that resembles natural language.

Leveraging Host Language Features: They can take advantage of the host language's features like type checking, code completion, and debugging tools.

Examples:

Ruby on Rails' Active Record (for database interactions)

jQuery (for DOM manipulation in JavaScript)

Kotlin's DSL for building HTML

External DSLs

Independent Languages: External DSLs are defined as separate languages with their own syntax and semantics, independent of any existing programming language.

Customizable Syntax: They offer greater flexibility in designing the language to closely match the domain's terminology and concepts.

Requires Parsing and Interpretation: They require building a parser to analyze the DSL code and an interpreter or compiler to execute or translate it.

Examples:

SQL (for database queries)

HTML (for web page structure)

ANTLR (for defining grammars)

Here's a table summarizing the key differences:

Feature	Internal DSL	External DSL
Implementation	Embedded in a host language	Separate language
Syntax	Restricted by host language syntax	Highly customizable
Parsing	No explicit parsing needed	Requires parser
Tooling	Leverages host language tools	Requires custom tools
Learning Curve	Easier for developers familiar with the host language	May require learning a new syntax
Flexibility	Less flexible in syntax design	More flexible

Choosing the Right Type:

The choice between internal and external DSLs depends on factors like the complexity of the domain, the need for custom syntax, the desired level of tooling support, and the expertise of the developers.

By understanding the characteristics of each type, you can make informed decisions about which approach best suits your needs when designing and implementing a DSL.

1.3 Benefits and Challenges

Benefits of DSLs

Increased Productivity:

Less code to write, leading to faster development cycles

Automation of repetitive tasks

Improved code readability and maintainability

Enhanced Communication:

Provides a shared language between developers and domain experts

Facilitates better understanding of requirements

Empowers domain experts to participate in software development

Reduced Complexity:

Abstraction of low-level details

Focus on domain-specific concepts

Domain-specific validation and error prevention

Increased Flexibility:

Tailored solutions for specific domains

Easier adaptation to evolving requirements

Improved code reusability

Challenges of DSLs

Initial Investment:

Time and effort required to design, implement, and learn a DSL

Potential need for specialized tools and infrastructure

Limited Scope:

DSLs are often specific to a particular domain and may not be applicable elsewhere

Can lead to fragmentation if multiple DSLs are used within a single system

Maintenance Overhead:

Requires ongoing maintenance and evolution of the DSL itself

Potential difficulty in finding developers with DSL expertise

Risk of Over-Engineering:

Temptation to create overly complex or specialized DSLs

Can lead to unnecessary abstraction and decreased understandability

Addressing the Challenges

It's important to acknowledge that while DSLs offer significant advantages, they also come with challenges. We can discuss strategies to mitigate these challenges, such as:

Starting Simple: Begin with a small, focused DSL and gradually expand it as needed.

Leveraging Existing Tools: Utilize existing tools and frameworks for DSL development to reduce the initial investment.

Prioritizing Usability: Focus on creating DSLs that are easy to learn and use for both developers and domain experts.

Maintaining Clear Documentation: Provide comprehensive documentation and examples to facilitate understanding and adoption.

By presenting a realistic view of the benefits and challenges, we can help readers make informed decisions about when and how to effectively utilize DSLs in their software projects.

Chapter 2

Key Concepts and Terminology

2.1 Abstract Syntax Trees (ASTs)

1. What is an AST?

Tree Structure: Explain that an AST is a tree-like data structure that represents the syntactic structure of source code.

Nodes and Edges: Describe how each node in the tree represents a construct in the code (e.g., expressions, statements, declarations), and the edges represent the relationships between these constructs.

Abstraction: Emphasize that ASTs abstract away concrete syntax details (like punctuation and whitespace) and focus on the essential structural elements.

2. Why are ASTs Important for DSLs?

Intermediate Representation: Explain how ASTs serve as an intermediate representation of the DSL code, bridging the gap between the textual input and its meaning.

Analysis and Manipulation: Demonstrate how ASTs can be traversed and analyzed to extract information, perform validation, and apply transformations.

Code Generation: Show how ASTs can be used to generate code in another language or format (e.g., generating machine code from a high-level DSL).

3. Constructing ASTs

Parsing: Introduce the concept of parsing, which is the process of converting source code into an AST.

Grammar Definition: Briefly touch on how grammars (like BNF or EBNF) are used to define the rules of the DSL's syntax.

Parser Generators: Mention tools like ANTLR and Lex/Yacc that can automatically generate parsers from grammar definitions.

4. Visualizing ASTs

Tree Diagrams: Include visual examples of ASTs to help readers grasp the concept.

Online Tools: Suggest online AST visualization tools that allow users to input code and see the corresponding AST.

5. Example with a Simple DSL

Define a Mini-Language: Create a simple DSL for a specific domain (e.g., a configuration language or a calculator language).

Illustrate Parsing: Show how a sample code snippet in the DSL is parsed into an AST.

Analyze the AST: Demonstrate how to traverse the AST to extract information or perform calculations.

By providing a clear and concise explanation of ASTs, with relevant examples and visualizations, we can ensure that readers gain a solid understanding of this crucial aspect of DSL development.

2.2 Grammars and Parsing

1. What are Grammars?

Formal Language Definition: Explain that grammars are formal systems used to define the syntax of a language, specifying the rules for how valid sentences or expressions can be constructed.

Types of Grammars: Briefly mention different types of grammars (e.g., context-free grammars, regular expressions) and their varying levels of expressiveness.

Grammar Notations: Introduce common notations like Backus-Naur Form (BNF) or Extended Backus-Naur Form (EBNF) for representing grammar rules.

2. The Role of Parsing

Analyzing Structure: Explain that parsing is the process of analyzing a sequence of tokens (like words or symbols) to determine its grammatical structure according to a given grammar.

Creating a Parse Tree: Describe how parsing produces a parse tree (or AST) that represents the hierarchical structure of the input.

Error Detection: Explain how parsers can detect syntax errors in the input and provide helpful error messages.

3. Parsing Techniques

Top-Down Parsing: Briefly explain top-down parsing, where the parser starts with the root of the parse tree and tries to match the input by applying grammar rules.

Bottom-Up Parsing: Briefly explain bottom-up parsing, where the parser starts with the input tokens and tries to build the parse tree from the bottom up.

Parser Generators: Mention tools like ANTLR, Lex/Yacc, and Bison that can automatically generate parsers from grammar definitions.

4. Illustrative Example

Simple Grammar: Define a simple grammar for a small DSL using BNF or EBNF notation.

Step-by-Step Parsing: Demonstrate how a parser would analyze a sample input string using the grammar, showing the construction of the parse tree.

Visualize the Process: Use diagrams to illustrate the parsing process and the resulting parse tree.

5. Practical Considerations

Error Handling: Discuss strategies for handling syntax errors and providing informative error messages.

Ambiguity: Briefly explain the concept of ambiguity in grammars and how it can affect parsing.

Performance: Touch on factors that can influence parsing performance, such as grammar complexity and input size.

By combining clear explanations, visual representations, and practical examples, we can make grammars and parsing accessible and engaging for our readers. This will provide them with a solid foundation for understanding how DSLs are structured and processed.

2.3 Semantic Analysis

1. What is Semantic Analysis?

Meaning and Context: Explain that semantic analysis examines the meaning of the code and ensures it makes sense within the context of the DSL and the domain it represents.

Beyond Syntax: Emphasize that while parsing checks the grammatical structure, semantic analysis goes deeper to verify the code's logic and consistency.

Example: Use a simple example to illustrate the difference. "Add 3 to apple" might be syntactically correct in a DSL, but semantically incorrect if "apple" is not defined as a numerical variable.

2. Tasks in Semantic Analysis

Symbol Table Construction: Describe how a symbol table is built to store information about variables, functions, and other language constructs.

Type Checking: Explain how the types of variables and expressions are checked for compatibility (e.g., preventing adding a number to a string).

Name Resolution: Discuss how references to variables and functions are resolved to their definitions.

Scope Checking: Explain how the scope of variables is verified to ensure they are accessed within their valid regions.

Domain-Specific Constraints: Emphasize that semantic analysis can enforce domain-specific rules and constraints, ensuring the code adheres to the domain's logic.

3. Semantic Errors

Examples: Provide examples of common semantic errors, such as:

Using an undeclared variable

Type mismatch in an operation

Calling a function with the wrong number of arguments

Violating domain-specific constraints

Error Reporting: Discuss how semantic analyzers should provide informative error messages to help users identify and correct the errors.

4. Relationship with ASTs

AST Traversal: Explain how semantic analysis often involves traversing the AST to gather information and perform checks.

Annotating the AST: Describe how the AST can be annotated with semantic information (e.g., type information) during the analysis.

5. Importance for DSLs

Ensuring Correctness: Highlight how semantic analysis helps ensure that DSL code is not only syntactically valid but also semantically meaningful within the domain.

Domain-Specific Validation: Emphasize how semantic analysis can enforce domain-specific rules and constraints, which is crucial for DSLs.

Improved Reliability: Explain how semantic analysis contributes to the reliability and correctness of DSL-based applications.

By clearly explaining the purpose and techniques of semantic analysis, we can equip our readers with the knowledge to build robust and reliable DSLs.

Chapter 3

Designing Effective DSLs

3.1 Understanding Your Domain

This is a critical first step! Before diving into the technicalities of DSL creation, it's crucial to have a deep understanding of the domain you're targeting. Here's how we can guide readers through this process:

1. Define the Domain Clearly

Scope and Boundaries: Encourage readers to clearly define the scope of their domain. What are the specific problems and tasks that the DSL will address? What are the boundaries of the domain?

Example: If building a DSL for web form validation, the domain might include input types, validation rules, error messages, and conditional logic. It might exclude aspects like server-side processing or database interactions.

2. Identify Key Concepts and Terminology

Domain Vocabulary: Guide readers to identify the essential concepts, entities, and relationships within the domain. What are the key terms and their definitions?

Example: In a DSL for financial trading, key concepts might include "stock," "order," "price," "volume," "limit order," "market order," and "portfolio."

3. Analyze Workflows and Tasks

Common Activities: Encourage readers to analyze the typical workflows and tasks performed within the domain. What are the common actions and operations? What are the typical sequences of steps?

Example: For a DSL for building user interfaces, common tasks might include creating layouts, adding widgets, defining event handlers, and styling elements.

4. Gather Domain Knowledge

Sources of Information: Suggest various sources for gathering domain knowledge, such as:

Domain Experts: Interviews, workshops, and shadowing

Existing Documentation: Manuals, specifications, and guidelines

Industry Standards: Relevant standards and best practices

Software Systems: Analyzing existing software in the domain

Example: For a DSL for network configuration, readers could consult network engineers, study network protocols, and analyze existing configuration files.

5. Create a Domain Model

Visual Representation: Encourage readers to create a visual representation of the domain model, such as a UML diagram or a concept map.

Relationships and Constraints: Highlight the importance of capturing relationships between concepts and any domain-specific constraints or rules.

Example: In a DSL for game development, a domain model might include entities like "character," "item," and "level," with relationships like "owns" (character owns item) and constraints like "maximum inventory size."

6. Refine and Validate the Model

Iterative Process: Emphasize that understanding the domain is an iterative process. The domain model should be refined and validated as new information is gathered and insights are gained.

Feedback from Experts: Encourage readers to seek feedback from domain experts to ensure the model accurately reflects the domain's complexities.

By guiding readers through this structured process of understanding their domain, we can empower them to create DSLs that are truly effective and aligned with the specific needs of their target users.

3.2 Data Processing and Analysis (SQL, R)

Great idea! SQL and R are excellent examples of DSLs specifically designed for data processing and analysis. Here's how we can present them in the book:

SQL (Structured Query Language)

Purpose: Explain that SQL is designed for managing and querying data in relational databases.

Key Features:

Declarative Style: Highlight that SQL is declarative, meaning you specify what data you want, not how to get it.

Data Manipulation: Cover core commands like `SELECT`, `INSERT`, `UPDATE`, `DELETE` for manipulating data.

Data Definition: Describe how SQL is used to define database schemas (tables, views, etc.) using commands like `CREATE`, `ALTER`, `DROP`.

Data Control: Briefly touch on SQL commands for access control and transaction management.

Example: Provide a clear example of a SQL query that retrieves specific data from a database table, demonstrating its conciseness and readability.

Purpose: Explain that R is a language and environment for statistical computing and graphics.

Key Features:

Data Structures: Describe R's powerful data structures like vectors, matrices, data frames, and lists.

Statistical Functions: Highlight R's vast collection of built-in functions for statistical analysis, modeling, and visualization.

Packages: Explain the concept of R packages that extend its functionality with specialized tools for various data analysis tasks.

Graphics: Showcase R's capabilities for creating high-quality visualizations and plots.

Example: Provide a simple R script that performs a statistical analysis on a dataset, demonstrating its expressive power and flexibility.

Comparing SQL and R

Different Strengths: Emphasize that while both are used for data analysis, they have different strengths. SQL excels at data manipulation within databases, while R is more powerful for statistical modeling and visualization.

Complementary Use: Explain how SQL and R can be used together. For example, SQL can extract and prepare data from a database, which can then be analyzed and visualized using R.

Other DSLs in Data Analysis

Briefly mention other DSLs relevant to data analysis, such as:

Data manipulation languages: dplyr (R), pandas (Python)

Data visualization languages: ggplot2 (R), matplotlib (Python)

Domain-specific query languages: Cypher (for graph databases), SPARQL (for RDF data)

By providing clear explanations and relevant examples of SQL and R, we can demonstrate the power and versatility of DSLs in the domain of data processing and analysis.

3.3 Prioritizing Usability

1. Why Usability Matters

Adoption and Productivity: Explain that a usable DSL leads to faster adoption, increased productivity, and fewer errors.

Reduced Learning Curve: A user-friendly DSL is easier to learn and master, making it accessible to a wider audience.

Maintainability: Usable DSLs result in code that is easier to read, understand, and maintain, reducing long-term costs.

User Satisfaction: Ultimately, a usable DSL leads to greater satisfaction for the developers and domain experts who use it.

2. Key Principles of DSL Usability

Clarity and Simplicity:

Intuitive Syntax: The DSL's syntax should be clear, concise, and closely aligned with the domain's terminology.

Minimalism: Avoid unnecessary complexity or features that could confuse users.

Consistency: Maintain consistency in naming conventions, syntax, and semantics throughout the DSL.

Readability and Understandability:

Meaningful Names: Use descriptive names for variables, functions, and other language constructs.

Clear Structure: Organize the DSL code in a logical and structured way to enhance readability.

Comments and Documentation: Encourage the use of comments and provide comprehensive documentation.

Error Prevention and Handling:

Domain-Specific Validation: Incorporate domain-specific constraints and validation rules to prevent errors.

Informative Error Messages: Provide clear and helpful error messages that guide users towards solutions.

Flexibility and Expressiveness:

Support for Common Tasks: Ensure the DSL can easily express the common tasks and workflows in the domain.

Extensibility: Allow for extensibility to accommodate future needs and evolving requirements.

3. Techniques for Evaluating Usability

Usability Testing:

Observe Users: Conduct usability testing sessions with target users to observe their interactions with the DSL.

Gather Feedback: Collect feedback on ease of use, clarity, and any difficulties encountered.

Expert Reviews:

Heuristic Evaluation: Have experts review the DSL design based on established usability heuristics.

Code Reviews: Conduct code reviews to identify potential usability issues in DSL code examples.

Surveys and Questionnaires:

Collect Quantitative Data: Use surveys to gather quantitative data on user satisfaction and perceived usability.

4. Iterative Design and Refinement

Continuous Improvement: Emphasize the importance of iterative design and continuous improvement based on user feedback and evaluation results.

Evolution of the DSL: The DSL should evolve over time to address usability issues and meet changing user needs.

By emphasizing usability and providing practical guidance on how to achieve it, we can help readers create DSLs that are not only powerful but also enjoyable and effective to use.

Chapter 4

Implementing DSLs with Internal DSLs

4.1 Leveraging Host Language Features

1. Syntactic Integration

Operator Overloading: Explain how operator overloading allows you to redefine the behavior of operators (like +, -, *) to work with domain-specific objects. This can make the DSL feel more natural and expressive.

Method Chaining: Show how method chaining can create fluent interfaces, where methods are called in sequence to form readable and expressive expressions.

Function Literals/Closures: Explain how function literals or closures can be used to define concise and reusable blocks of code within the DSL.

2. Type System

Static Typing: If the host language has static typing, explain how it can be used to enforce domain-specific constraints and catch errors at compile time.

Type Inference: Discuss how type inference can reduce the need for explicit type declarations, making the DSL code more concise.

Custom Types: Show how to define custom types or classes to represent domain-specific concepts and data structures.

3. Libraries and Frameworks

Existing Functionality: Encourage readers to leverage existing libraries and frameworks in the host language to avoid reinventing the wheel.

Domain-Specific Libraries: If there are libraries specifically relevant to the domain, explain how they can be integrated into the DSL.

Metaprogramming: If the host language supports metaprogramming, discuss how it can be used to generate code or manipulate the DSL's structure at compile time.

4. Tooling

IDEs and Editors: Explain how existing IDEs and editors can provide code completion, syntax highlighting, and debugging support for the DSL.

Testing Frameworks: Show how existing testing frameworks can be used to write unit tests and integration tests for the DSL code.

Build Tools: Discuss how build tools can be used to automate the compilation and packaging of DSL-based applications.

5. Examples

Concrete Examples: Provide concrete examples in popular languages like Java, Python, or Kotlin, demonstrating how specific host language features are used to create expressive and powerful DSLs.

Real-world DSLs: Analyze real-world DSLs built within existing languages, highlighting how they leverage host language features to achieve their goals.

By effectively leveraging host language features, readers can create internal DSLs that are not only powerful and expressive but also well-integrated with the existing ecosystem, making them easier to adopt and maintain.

4.2 API Design for DSLs

1. DSL-Specific API Design Considerations

Domain Alignment: Emphasize that the API should closely reflect the domain's concepts and terminology. Method names, parameters, and return types should use domain-specific languagwhenever possible.

Fluent Interfaces: Encourage the use of method chaining and fluent interfaces to create expressive and readable DSL code.

Conciseness: Strive for conciseness in the API design. Minimize the number of required parameters and make use of default values where appropriate.

Consistency: Maintain consistency in naming conventions, parameter order, and error handling throughout the API.

Discoverability: Design the API to be easily discoverable. Use clear and descriptive names, and provide good documentation and examples.

2. API Design Principles

Abstraction: Hide implementation details and complexity behind a clean and simple API.

Encapsulation: Group related functionality into cohesive classes or modules.

Information Hiding: Minimize the exposure of internal data structures and implementation details.

Loose Coupling: Minimize dependencies between different parts of the API to promote flexibility and maintainability.

Single Responsibility Principle: Each class or method should have a clear and well-defined responsibility.

3. API Design Patterns

Builder Pattern: Useful for creating complex objects step-by-step, especially when there are many optional parameters.

Factory Pattern: Provides a way to create objects without exposing the instantiation logic to the DSL user.

Strategy Pattern: Allows for the selection of different algorithms or behaviors at runtime.

Decorator Pattern: Adds responsibilities to objects dynamically without modifying their structure.

4. Documentation and Examples

Comprehensive Documentation: Provide clear and comprehensive documentation for the API, including explanations of each method, parameter, and return type.

Code Examples: Include plenty of code examples to demonstrate how to use the API to create DSL expressions.

Tutorials and Guides: Consider creating tutorials and guides that walk users through building more complex DSL constructs.

5. Evolution and Versioning

API Stability: Strive to maintain API stability to avoid breaking changes for DSL users.

Versioning: If breaking changes are necessary, introduce new API versions and provide migration guides.

Deprecation: Clearly mark deprecated methods and provide alternatives to encourage users to update their code.

By guiding readers through these API design considerations and best practices, we can empower them to create internal DSLs that are not only powerful and expressive but also easy to use and maintain.

4.3 Examples in Popular Languages (Java, Python, etc.)

You're right, concrete examples are key to understanding how internal DSLs work in practice! Here are some examples in popular languages, showcasing different approaches and features:

Java

Fluent Interfaces with Method Chaining:

Java

```
// Building an HTML table using a Java DSL
HtmlTable table = new HtmlTable()
    .withRows(3)
    .withColumns(2)
    .addRow()
        .addCell("Name")
        .addCell("Age")
    .addRow()
        .addCell("John Doe")
        .addCell("30");
```

Using Lambdas for Concise Expressions:

Java

```
// Defining validation rules for a form field
Validator validator = new Validator()
    .addRule(field -> field.length() > 0, "Field cannot be empty")
    .addRule(field -> field.matches("[a-zA-Z]+"), "Field must contain only letters");
```

Python

Leveraging Decorators for Domain-Specific Annotations:

Python

```python
# Defining a route in a web framework
@route("/users/<id>")
def get_user(id):
    # ...
```

Using Context Managers for Resource Management:

Python

```python
# Working with a database connection
with database.connect() as connection:
    cursor = connection.cursor()
    # ... perform database operations ...
```

Kotlin

Type-Safe Builders for Hierarchical Structures:

Kotlin

```kotlin
// Building an HTML form using Kotlin DSL
html {
  form {
    input(type = "text", name = "username")
    input(type = "password", name = "password")
    button(type = "submit") { +"Login" }
  }
```

}

Operator Overloading for Expressive Syntax:

Kotlin

```
// Defining arithmetic operations on custom objects
data class Vector(val x: Int, val y: Int) {
    operator fun plus(other: Vector): Vector = Vector(x + other.x, y + other.y)
}

val v1 = Vector(1, 2)
val v2 = Vector(3, 4)
val v3 = v1 + v2  // v3 will be Vector(4, 6)
```

Key Takeaways

Language Features: These examples demonstrate how language features like method chaining, lambdas, decorators, and operator overloading can be used to create expressive and readable DSLs.

Domain Alignment: The API design in these examples closely aligns with the domain terminology, making the DSL code feel natural and intuitive.

Conciseness and Readability: The DSL code is concise and readable, reducing boilerplate and improving maintainability.

By showcasing these concrete examples, we can help readers understand how to effectively leverage the features of their chosen language to create powerful and usable internal DSLs.

Chapter 5

Creating External DSLs

5.1 Lexical Analysis and Parsing Techniques

1. Lexical Analysis (Scanning)

Tokenization: Explain that lexical analysis breaks down the input text into a sequence of tokens, which are the basic building blocks of the language (e.g., keywords, identifiers, operators, literals).

Regular Expressions: Introduce regular expressions as a powerful tool for defining patterns that match different types of tokens.

Lexical Analyzer: Describe the role of a lexical analyzer (or scanner) in reading the input and generating a stream of tokens.

2. Parsing (Syntax Analysis)

Grammar Rules: Explain how a formal grammar defines the rules for how tokens can be combined to form valid expressions and statements in the DSL.

Parse Tree (AST): Describe how parsing produces a parse tree (or AST) that represents the hierarchical structure of the input according to the grammar.

Parser: Explain the role of a parser in analyzing the token stream and constructing the parse tree.

3. Parsing Techniques

Top-Down Parsing:

Recursive Descent: Explain this common top-down technique, where the parser uses recursive functions to match grammar rules.

LL Parsing: Briefly mention LL parsers, which use a lookahead buffer to predict which rule to apply.

Bottom-Up Parsing:

Shift-Reduce Parsing: Explain this common bottom-up technique, where the parser shifts tokens onto a stack and reduces them based on grammar rules.

LR Parsing: Briefly mention LR parsers, which are more powerful and can handle a wider range of grammars.

4. Parser Generators

ANTLR: Introduce ANTLR as a popular parser generator that can automatically generate lexers and parsers from grammar definitions.

Other Tools: Mention other parser generators like Lex/Yacc, Bison, and JavaCC.

5. Error Handling

Lexical Errors: Discuss how to handle lexical errors, such as invalid characters or unrecognized tokens.

Syntax Errors: Explain how to handle syntax errors, such as missing tokens or incorrect order of tokens.

Error Reporting: Emphasize the importance of providing informative error messages that help users identify and correct the errors.

6. Practical Considerations

Grammar Design: Discuss the importance of designing a clear and unambiguous grammar to avoid parsing conflicts.

Performance: Touch on factors that can influence parsing performance, such as grammar complexity and input size.

Example

Simple DSL: Define a simple DSL with a corresponding grammar (e.g., a calculator language or a configuration file format).

Lexical Analysis: Show how the input text is tokenized.

Parsing: Illustrate how a parser would analyze the tokens and construct the parse tree.

By providing a clear explanation of lexical analysis and parsing techniques, combined with practical examples and tools, we can equip readers with the knowledge to build robust and efficient parsers for their external DSLs.

5.2 Building Interpreters and Compilers

This is where the rubber meets the road for external DSLs! Once you have the parsed structure (AST) of your DSL code, you need a way to execute it or translate it into something executable. Here's how we can guide readers through the fascinating world of interpreters and compilers:

1. Interpreters

Direct Execution: Explain that an interpreter directly executes the DSL code, typically by traversing the AST and performing actions based on the nodes encountered.

Runtime Environment: Discuss the concept of a runtime environment that provides the necessary context for execution, including variable storage, function definitions, and built-in operations.

Advantages:

Simplicity: Interpreters are often simpler to implement than compilers.

Interactivity: They allow for interactive execution and debugging of the DSL code.

Portability: The same interpreter can often run on different platforms.

Disadvantages:

Performance: Interpreted code is generally slower than compiled code.

Dynamic Typing: Dynamically typed DSLs might have runtime errors that could have been caught by a compiler.

2. Compilers

Translation to Target Language: Explain that a compiler translates the DSL code into another language, typically a lower-level language like assembly or machine code, or even another high-level language.

Compilation Phases: Briefly describe the typical phases of compilation: lexical analysis, parsing, semantic analysis, optimization, and code generation.

Advantages:

Performance: Compiled code generally runs faster than interpreted code.

Optimization: Compilers can perform optimizations to improve the efficiency of the generated code.

Static Analysis: Compilers can perform static analysis to catch errors and potential issues before runtime.

Disadvantages:

Complexity: Compilers are generally more complex to implement than interpreters.

Platform Dependence: Compiled code is often specific to a particular platform or architecture.

3. Choosing the Right Approach

Performance vs. Simplicity: Discuss the trade-off between performance and simplicity when choosing between an interpreter and a compiler.

Domain Requirements: Consider the specific requirements of the domain, such as the need for interactivity, portability, or performance.

Existing Tools: Explore existing tools and libraries that can assist in building interpreters or compilers.

4. Example Implementation

Simple DSL: Choose a simple DSL (e.g., a calculator language) and illustrate how to build both an interpreter and a compiler for it.

Interpreter: Show how the interpreter traverses the AST and performs calculations.

Compiler: Show how the compiler translates the DSL code into a target language (e.g., generating assembly code).

5. Advanced Topics (Optional)

Just-in-Time (JIT) Compilation: Briefly introduce JIT compilation as a technique that combines aspects of both interpreters and compilers.

Virtual Machines: Discuss the role of virtual machines in executing compiled code.

Optimization Techniques: Mention common compiler optimization techniques.

By providing clear explanations, practical examples, and a discussion of the trade-offs involved, we can guide readers in making informed decisions about building interpreters and compilers for their external DSLs.

5.3 Code Generation Strategies

Code generation is the final act in bringing an external DSL to life! It's where the abstract representation of the DSL code is transformed into something that a machine can understand and execute. Here's how we can guide readers through different code generation strategies:

1. Target Language Selection

Assembly Language: Discuss generating assembly code for specific processors, offering fine-grained control but requiring platform-specific knowledge.

Bytecode: Explain generating bytecode for virtual machines (like Java's JVM or Python's PVM), providing portability but potentially sacrificing some performance.

High-Level Languages: Explore translating the DSL into another high-level language (like C++, Java, or Python), leveraging existing compilers and ecosystems.

2. Code Generation Approaches

Template-Based:

Predefined Templates: Explain using predefined code templates for common DSL constructs, filling in the blanks with specific values from the AST.

Example: Generating HTML from a DSL for web page design.

Tree Walking:

Recursive Traversal: Describe traversing the AST recursively and generating code for each node based on its type and attributes.

Example: Generating SQL queries from a DSL for database interaction.

Model-Driven:

Code from Models: Explain generating code from higher-level models or domain-specific representations.

Example: Generating code from UML diagrams or domain-specific ontologies.

3. Optimizations

Basic Optimizations: Discuss simple optimizations like constant folding, dead code elimination, and common subexpression elimination.

DSL-Specific Optimizations: Explore optimizations tailored to the specific domain and the characteristics of the DSL.

Trade-offs: Explain the trade-off between optimization effort and the potential performance gains.

4. Code Generation Tools

String Templates: Introduce string template engines (like StringTemplate or Jinja) for generating code from templates.

Code Generation Frameworks: Mention frameworks that provide support for code generation tasks (like ANTLR's code generation features or Eclipse Xtext).

5. Practical Considerations

Error Handling: Discuss how to handle errors during code generation and provide informative error messages.

Code Formatting: Emphasize the importance of generating well-formatted and readable code.

Testing: Explain how to test the generated code to ensure its correctness and efficiency.

Example

Simple DSL: Choose a simple DSL (e.g., a configuration language) and illustrate different code generation strategies.

Template-Based: Show how to use templates to generate configuration files.

Tree Walking: Demonstrate how to traverse the AST and generate equivalent code in a target language.

By providing a clear understanding of code generation strategies, tools, and best practices, we can empower readers to effectively translate their DSLs into executable code, realizing the full potential of their custom languages.

Chapter 6

Advanced DSL Techniques

6.1 Metaprogramming and Macros

Metaprogramming and macros are powerful tools that can significantly enhance the expressiveness and flexibility of DSLs. They allow you to manipulate code as data and generate code dynamically, enabling you to extend the language and create abstractions tailored to your specific domain. Here's how we can explain these concepts in the book:

1. Metaprogramming

Code as Data: Explain the core idea of metaprogramming, which is treating code as data that can be manipulated and transformed by programs.

Reflection: Discuss reflection as a common metaprogramming technique that allows programs to examine and modify their own structure and behavior at runtime.

Advantages:

Increased Abstraction: Metaprogramming enables the creation of higher-level abstractions and domain-specific constructs.

Code Generation: It allows for dynamic code generation, reducing boilerplate and improving code reuse.

Extensibility: It enables extending the language with new features and syntax.

Examples:

Generating code: Creating code generators that produce code based on models or specifications.

Modifying behavior: Using decorators or annotations to modify the behavior of existing code.

2. Macros

Code Transformation: Explain that macros are a form of metaprogramming that allows you to transform code at compile time.

Syntax Extension: Show how macros can be used to extend the syntax of the language with new constructs or shorthand notations.

Hygienic Macros: Discuss the importance of hygienic macros, which prevent unintended variable capture and name clashes.

Advantages:

Domain-Specific Syntax: Macros enable the creation of syntax that closely matches the domain's terminology and concepts.

Code Simplification: They can simplify repetitive code patterns and reduce boilerplate.

Compile-Time Optimization: Macros can perform optimizations at compile time, potentially improving performance.

Examples:

Creating DSLs: Using macros to define the syntax and semantics of a new DSL.

Simplifying code: Creating macros that generate commonly used code patterns.

3. Lisp Macros

Powerful Macro System: Highlight Lisp's powerful macro system, which allows for extensive code manipulation and transformation.

Code as Lists: Explain how Lisp code is represented as lists, making it particularly well-suited for metaprogramming.

Example: Show a simple Lisp macro that defines a new looping construct.

4. Macros in Other Languages

C/C++ Macros: Discuss the preprocessor macros in C/C++, noting their limitations and potential pitfalls.

Rust Macros: Introduce Rust's macro system, which offers more safety and expressiveness than C/C++ macros.

Template Metaprogramming: Briefly explain template metaprogramming in C++, which allows for compile-time code generation.

5. Practical Considerations

Debugging: Discuss the challenges of debugging macro-generated code and suggest strategies for effective debugging.

Maintainability: Emphasize the importance of writing clear and well-documented macros to ensure maintainability.

Overuse: Caution against overusing macros, as they can make code harder to understand if used excessively.

By providing a clear explanation of metaprogramming and macros, with relevant examples and practical considerations, we can empower readers to leverage these powerful techniques to create expressive and effective DSLs.

6.2 Domain-Specific Modeling (DSM)

Domain-Specific Modeling (DSM) takes DSLs to the next level! It's about creating visual or textual models that directly represent the concepts and relationships in a specific domain, and then using those models to generate code or other artifacts. Here's how we can explain DSM in the book:

1. What is DSM?

Raising the Level of Abstraction: Explain that DSM raises the level of abstraction beyond code, allowing developers to work with models that are closer to the domain expert's understanding.

Visual or Textual Models: Describe how DSM uses visual notations (like diagrams) or textual languages to represent domain-specific concepts and relationships.

Code Generation: Emphasize that DSM often involves generating code from the models, automating a significant part of the development process.

2. Benefits of DSM

Improved Communication: DSM facilitates communication between developers and domain experts by providing a shared visual or textual language.

Increased Productivity: Automating code generation reduces development time and effort.

Reduced Errors: Models can be validated and checked for consistency, reducing the likelihood of errors in the generated code.

Improved Maintainability: Changes to the system can be made at the model level, simplifying maintenance and evolution.

3. DSM Tools and Languages

Graphical Modeling Tools: Introduce popular graphical modeling tools like Eclipse Sirius, MetaEdit+, and Visual Paradigm.

Textual DSM Languages: Mention textual DSM languages like JetBrains MPS and Xtext.

Domain-Specific Languages: Explain how DSLs are often used as the foundation for creating DSM languages.

4. DSM Process

Domain Analysis: Emphasize the importance of thorough domain analysis to identify key concepts and relationships.

Metamodel Definition: Explain the concept of a metamodel, which defines the structure and rules of the domain-specific models.

Model Creation: Describe how domain experts and developers create models using the chosen DSM language or tool.

Model Validation: Discuss techniques for validating models to ensure their correctness and consistency.

Code Generation: Explain how code generators transform models into executable code.

5. Example

Simple Domain: Choose a simple domain (e.g., designing user interfaces) and illustrate the DSM process.

Metamodel: Define a metamodel for the domain, including concepts like "window," "button," and "layout."

Model: Create a visual or textual model of a user interface using the metamodel.

Code Generation: Show how code (e.g., HTML, JavaScript) can be generated from the model.

6. Advanced Concepts (Optional)

Model Transformations: Briefly discuss model transformations, which allow for manipulating and converting models.

Model-Driven Architecture (MDA): Mention MDA as a broader approach to software development that emphasizes the use of models.

By providing a clear explanation of DSM, its benefits, tools, and processes, we can empower readers to explore this powerful approach to software development and leverage it to create more effective and maintainable systems.

6.3 Testing and Debugging DSLs

Testing and debugging are critical aspects of DSL development, ensuring that your language works as intended and that programs written in it are correct and reliable. Here's how we can guide readers through effective testing and debugging strategies for DSLs:

1. Testing DSLs

Types of Tests:

Unit Tests: Test individual components of the DSL implementation (parser, interpreter, code generator) in isolation.

Integration Tests: Test the interaction between different components of the DSL.

Acceptance Tests: Test the DSL as a whole against real-world scenarios and user expectations.

Test Cases:

Valid Input: Test with valid DSL code to ensure it's parsed and interpreted correctly.

Invalid Input: Test with invalid DSL code to ensure errors are detected and reported accurately.

Edge Cases: Test with boundary conditions and unusual inputs to uncover potential issues.

Domain-Specific Tests: Design tests that specifically target the domain's rules and constraints.

Testing Frameworks:

Leverage Existing Frameworks: Encourage the use of existing testing frameworks (JUnit for Java, pytest for Python, etc.) to organize and execute tests.

DSL-Specific Testing Tools: If applicable, mention any DSL-specific testing tools or frameworks that provide additional support.

2. Debugging DSLs

Debugging Techniques:

Print Statements/Logging: Use print statements or logging to trace the execution of the DSL code and inspect intermediate values.

Debuggers: If available, use debuggers to step through the code, set breakpoints, and inspect variables.

Visualization: Visualize the AST or other intermediate representations to understand the structure of the code.

Testing Tools: Leverage testing frameworks to isolate and reproduce errors.

Debugging Challenges:

Abstraction: The level of abstraction in DSLs can make it harder to trace the execution flow.

Generated Code: Debugging generated code can be challenging, as it might not directly correspond to the original DSL code.

Debugging Strategies:

Start Simple: Begin with simple test cases and gradually increase complexity.

Isolate Errors: Use testing and debugging techniques to isolate the source of errors.

Inspect Intermediate Representations: Examine the AST or other intermediate data structures to understand the code's transformation.

3. Tools and Techniques

Test-Driven Development (TDD): Encourage the use of TDD to write tests before implementing the DSL, ensuring testability from the start.

Debugging Aids: If applicable, mention any DSL-specific debugging aids or tools that can help diagnose and fix errors.

Static Analysis: Discuss the use of static analysis tools to identify potential issues in the DSL code before runtime.

4. Example

Simple DSL: Choose a simple DSL and demonstrate how to write unit tests and debug common errors.

Test Cases: Show examples of test cases for valid and invalid input, edge cases, and domain-specific rules.

Debugging Process: Illustrate the debugging process using print statements, debuggers, or visualization tools.

By providing clear guidance on testing and debugging techniques, tools, and strategies, we can help readers create robust and reliable DSLs and ensure that their DSL-based applications function as expected.

Chapter 7

DSLs for Specific Domains

7.1 Web Development (HTML, CSS)

HTML (HyperText Markup Language)

Purpose: Explain that HTML is designed to define the structure and content of web pages.

Key Features:

Tags and Elements: Describe how HTML uses tags to mark up different elements of a web page (headings, paragraphs, images, links, etc.).

Attributes: Explain how attributes provide additional information about elements (e.g., source of an image, target of a link).

Semantic Markup: Emphasize the importance of using semantic HTML5 tags to convey the meaning of content (e.g., `<article>`, `<nav>`, `<aside>`).

Example: Provide a simple HTML code snippet that demonstrates the basic structure of a web page, including headings, paragraphs, and an image.

CSS (Cascading Style Sheets)

Purpose: Explain that CSS is designed to control the visual presentation and layout of web pages.

Key Features:

Selectors: Describe how CSS selectors target specific HTML elements to apply styles.

Properties and Values: Explain how CSS properties (e.g., `color`, `font-size`, `margin`) and their values define the styles.

Cascading and Inheritance: Discuss the concept of cascading and inheritance, which determine how styles are applied when multiple rules match an element.

Example: Provide a CSS code snippet that demonstrates how to style a paragraph with a specific font, color, and margin.

HTML and CSS as DSLs

Domain-Specific Vocabulary: Highlight how HTML and CSS provide a domain-specific vocabulary for web page creation.

Declarative Style: Emphasize that both languages are declarative, meaning you specify what the web page should look like, not how to achieve it.

Abstraction: Explain how they abstract away the underlying complexities of rendering web pages in different browsers.

Beyond HTML and CSS

JavaScript: Briefly mention JavaScript as the programming language used to add interactivity and dynamic behavior to web pages.

Web Frameworks: Discuss how web frameworks (React, Angular, Vue.js) build upon HTML, CSS, and JavaScript to provide higher-level abstractions and tools for web development.

Example

Simple Web Page: Create a simple web page that demonstrates the use of HTML and CSS to structure and style content.

HTML Structure: Show how to use HTML tags to create headings, paragraphs, and an image.

CSS Styling: Show how to use CSS selectors and properties to style the elements with different colors, fonts, and layouts.

By showcasing HTML and CSS as prime examples of DSLs in web development, we can demonstrate how DSLs can simplify complex tasks and empower developers to create sophisticated applications with ease.

7.2 Data Processing and Analysis (SQL, R)

SQL (Structured Query Language)

Purpose: Explain that SQL is designed for managing and querying data in relational databases. It allows users to interact with databases to retrieve, manipulate, and define data.

Key Features:

Declarative Style: Emphasize that SQL is declarative, meaning you specify *what* data you want, not *how* to get it. This makes it easier to read and write complex queries.

Data Manipulation: Cover core commands like `SELECT`, `INSERT`, `UPDATE`, `DELETE` for retrieving, adding, modifying, and removing data.

Data Definition: Describe how SQL defines database schemas (tables, views, etc.) using commands like `CREATE`, `ALTER`, `DROP`.

Data Control: Briefly touch on SQL commands for access control (e.g., granting permissions) and transaction management (e.g., ensuring data consistency).

Example: Provide a clear example of a SQL query that retrieves specific data from a database table, demonstrating its conciseness and readability. For example:

SQL

```
SELECT name, age
 FROM employees
 WHERE department = 'Sales' AND age > 30;
```

R

Purpose: Explain that R is a language and environment specifically designed for statistical computing and graphics. It's widely used by statisticians and data scientists for data analysis and visualization.

Key Features:

Data Structures: Describe R's powerful data structures like vectors, matrices, data frames, and lists, which are optimized for handling data.

Statistical Functions: Highlight R's vast collection of built-in functions for statistical analysis (t-tests, regressions, etc.), modeling, and visualization.

Packages: Explain the concept of R packages that extend its functionality with specialized tools for various data analysis tasks (e.g., `ggplot2` for visualization, `dplyr` for data manipulation).

Graphics: Showcase R's capabilities for creating high-quality visualizations and plots to gain insights from data.

Example: Provide a simple R script that performs a statistical analysis on a dataset, demonstrating its expressive power and flexibility. For example:

Code snippet

```
# Calculate the mean of a vector
data <- c(1, 2, 3, 4, 5)
```

```
mean(data)
```

Comparing SQL and R

Different Strengths: Emphasize that while both are used for data analysis, they have different strengths. SQL excels at data manipulation within databases, while R is more powerful for statistical modeling, visualization, and advanced analytics.

Complementary Use: Explain how SQL and R can be used together. For example, SQL can extract and prepare data from a database, which can then be analyzed and visualized using R.

Other DSLs in Data Analysis

Briefly mention other DSLs relevant to data analysis, such as:

Data manipulation languages: dplyr (R), pandas (Python)

Data visualization languages: ggplot2 (R), matplotlib (Python)

Domain-specific query languages: Cypher (for graph databases), SPARQL (for RDF data)

By providing clear explanations and relevant examples of SQL and R, we can demonstrate the power and versatility of DSLs in the domain of data processing and analysis.

7.3 DevOps and Infrastructure Automation

1. DevOps Principles

Collaboration and Automation: Explain how DevOps emphasizes collaboration between development and operations teams, with automation as a key enabler.

Infrastructure as Code (IaC): Introduce IaC as the practice of managing and provisioning infrastructure through code rather than manual processes.

Continuous Integration and Continuous Delivery (CI/CD): Describe CI/CD pipelines that automate the building, testing, and deployment of applications.

2. DSLs for Infrastructure Automation

Configuration Management:

Tools like Ansible, Puppet, and Chef: Explain how these tools use DSLs to define the desired state of infrastructure (servers, networks, applications), automating configuration and deployment tasks.

Example: Show an Ansible playbook that defines the steps to install and configure a web server.

Provisioning:

Tools like Terraform and CloudFormation: Describe how these tools use DSLs to define infrastructure resources (virtual machines, storage, networks) in cloud environments.

Example: Show a Terraform configuration file that defines a virtual machine with specific properties.

Container Orchestration:

Kubernetes: Explain how Kubernetes uses a DSL to define and manage containerized applications, automating deployment, scaling, and networking.

Example: Show a Kubernetes YAML file that defines a deployment and a service.

3. Benefits of DSLs in DevOps

Increased Efficiency: Automation through DSLs reduces manual effort and accelerates infrastructure management.

Improved Consistency: DSLs ensure that infrastructure is provisioned and configured consistently across different environments.

Reduced Errors: Automated processes minimize the risk of human error in manual configuration.

Increased Scalability: DSLs enable the management of large and complex infrastructure with ease.

Version Control: Infrastructure defined as code can be version-controlled, tracked, and rolled back if needed.

4. Examples

Building a CI/CD Pipeline: Show how to use DSLs in tools like Jenkins or GitLab CI to define a CI/CD pipeline that automates the build, test, and deployment process.

Deploying to the Cloud: Demonstrate how to use Terraform or CloudFormation to provision infrastructure on cloud platforms like AWS, Azure, or GCP.

Managing a Kubernetes Cluster: Show how to use Kubernetes YAML files to define and deploy applications on a Kubernetes cluster.

5. Advanced Topics (Optional)

Serverless Computing: Discuss how DSLs can be used to define and deploy serverless functions and applications.

Infrastructure Testing: Explain how to write tests for infrastructure code to ensure its correctness and reliability.

By showcasing the power of DSLs in DevOps and infrastructure automation, we can demonstrate how these tools can help organizations achieve faster, more reliable, and more efficient software delivery.

Chapter 8

DSLs for Improved Productivity

8.1 Code Generation and Automation

1. The Power of Code Generation

Automation of Repetitive Tasks: Explain how code generation automates the creation of repetitive code patterns, reducing manual effort and the potential for errors.

Increased Productivity: By generating code instead of writing it by hand, developers can focus on more complex and creative tasks.

Improved Consistency: Generated code adheres to predefined templates and rules, ensuring consistency and reducing the risk of inconsistencies.

Reduced Errors: Automated code generation minimizes the chance of human errors that can occur during manual coding.

Enhanced Maintainability: Changes to the system can be made at the model or DSL level, and the code can be regenerated, simplifying maintenance.

2. DSLs as a Foundation for Code Generation

Domain-Specific Abstractions: Explain how DSLs provide domain-specific abstractions that can be used to generate code tailored to the specific needs of the domain.

Model-Driven Code Generation: Discuss how DSLs can be used to create models or specifications that are then used to generate code.

Example: Show how a DSL for defining user interfaces can be used to generate HTML, CSS, and JavaScript code.

3. Code Generation Techniques

Template-Based Code Generation: Explain how templates can be used to define code patterns with placeholders that are filled in with specific values from the DSL code or model.

Tree-Walking Code Generation: Describe how the AST of the DSL code can be traversed to generate code based on the structure and attributes of the nodes.

Model-Driven Code Generation: Discuss how models created using DSLs can be transformed into code using code generators.

4. Code Generation Tools

Template Engines: Introduce template engines (like StringTemplate, Jinja, or Velocity) that can be used to generate code from templates.

Code Generation Frameworks: Mention frameworks like ANTLR or Xtext that provide support for code generation tasks.

IDEs with Code Generation Features: Discuss how some IDEs offer built-in code generation features that can be customized for specific DSLs.

5. Automation Beyond Code Generation

Build Automation: Explain how DSLs can be used to automate build processes, including compilation, testing, and packaging.

Deployment Automation: Discuss how DSLs can be used to automate the deployment of applications to various environments.

Infrastructure Automation: Mention how DSLs are used in tools like Ansible, Puppet, and Terraform to automate infrastructure provisioning and management.

6. Examples

Generating Web Applications: Show how a DSL can be used to generate a complete web application, including HTML, CSS, and JavaScript code, from a high-level description.

Automating Database Access: Demonstrate how a DSL can be used to generate code for accessing and manipulating data in a database.

Creating Configuration Files: Show how a DSL can be used to generate configuration files for various applications or systems.

7. Benefits and Challenges

Benefits: Reiterate the benefits of code generation and automation, including increased productivity, reduced errors, and improved maintainability.

Challenges: Discuss the challenges of code generation, such as the initial investment in creating the DSL and code generator, and the potential for complexity in managing generated code.

By providing a clear understanding of code generation techniques, tools, and best practices, we can empower readers to effectively automate repetitive tasks, improve code quality, and accelerate software development using DSLs.

8.2 Reducing Boilerplate Code

1. The Problem with Boilerplate Code

Tedious and Repetitive: Explain how boilerplate code often involves writing the same code structures repeatedly, such as getters/setters, constructors, or try-catch blocks.

Error-Prone: Manual repetition increases the risk of typos and inconsistencies, leading to errors.

Reduced Readability: Boilerplate code clutters the codebase, making it harder to read and understand the essential logic.

Maintenance Overhead: Changes to boilerplate code often have to be replicated across multiple places, increasing maintenance effort.

2. How DSLs Reduce Boilerplate

Abstraction: DSLs provide higher-level abstractions that hide the underlying boilerplate code.

Code Generation: DSLs can generate boilerplate code automatically, freeing developers from writing it manually.

Domain-Specific Constructs: DSLs can introduce domain-specific constructs that encapsulate common patterns and idioms, reducing the need for verbose code.

3. Examples

Object-Oriented Programming:

Getters/Setters: Show how DSLs can generate getters and setters for object properties, eliminating the need to write them by hand.

Constructors: Demonstrate how DSLs can generate constructors with various parameters, simplifying object creation.

Data Access:

Database Queries: Explain how DSLs like SQL abstract away the complexities of database interaction, reducing the amount of code needed to perform queries.

Object-Relational Mapping (ORM): Discuss how ORMs use DSLs to map objects to database tables, eliminating the need for manual SQL queries.

Web Development:

HTML Generation: Show how DSLs can generate HTML code from higher-level descriptions, reducing the need to write HTML tags manually.

Form Handling: Demonstrate how DSLs can simplify form handling by generating code for validation, data binding, and submission.

4. Benefits of Reducing Boilerplate

Increased Productivity: Less time spent writing boilerplate code means more time for focusing on core logic and delivering value.

Improved Code Readability: Cleaner code with less boilerplate is easier to read, understand, and maintain.

Reduced Errors: Automated code generation minimizes the risk of errors introduced by manual repetition.

Faster Development: Less code to write means faster development cycles and quicker time-to-market.

5. Tools and Techniques

Metaprogramming: Discuss how metaprogramming techniques can be used to generate boilerplate code dynamically.

Macros: Explain how macros can be used to create shorthand notations for common code patterns.

Code Generation Frameworks: Mention frameworks like Lombok (for Java) or Rails (for Ruby) that provide built-in support for reducing boilerplate.

By highlighting the problem of boilerplate code and demonstrating how DSLs can effectively address it, we can show readers how DSLs can lead to cleaner, more efficient, and more maintainable codebases.

8.3 Improving Code Readability and Maintainability

1. The Importance of Readability

Understanding Code: Explain how readable code is easier to understand, both for the original developer and for others who may need to work on it later.

Reduced Cognitive Load: Readable code reduces the mental effort required to understand its logic, making it easier to work with and modify.

Faster Debugging: When code is easy to read, it's easier to identify and fix errors.

Improved Collaboration: Readable code facilitates collaboration among team members, as everyone can easily understand what the code does.

2. The Importance of Maintainability

Adapting to Change: Maintainable code is easier to modify and adapt to changing requirements.

Reduced Bugs: Well-maintained code is less prone to bugs and errors.

Longer Lifespan: Maintainable code can have a longer lifespan, as it can be easily updated and extended.

Reduced Costs: Maintainability reduces the long-term costs of software development by making it easier and less expensive to make changes.

3. How DSLs Improve Readability

Domain-Specific Vocabulary: DSLs use terminology and concepts that are familiar to domain experts, making the code more intuitive and easier to understand.

Abstraction: DSLs hide low-level details and complexity, presenting a cleaner and more concise view of the logic.

Expressive Syntax: DSLs can be designed with a syntax that is more expressive and readable than general-purpose languages.

4. How DSLs Improve Maintainability

Modularity: DSLs can promote modularity by encapsulating domain-specific logic into reusable components.

Code Generation: DSLs can generate code automatically, ensuring consistency and reducing the risk of errors introduced by manual coding.

Separation of Concerns: DSLs can separate domain logic from technical details, making it easier to modify and evolve the system.

5. Examples

Configuration Files: Show how a DSL for configuration files can improve readability compared to traditional configuration formats.

Business Rules: Demonstrate how a DSL for expressing business rules can make them more understandable and maintainable.

Data Transformation: Explain how a DSL for data transformation can simplify complex data manipulation tasks.

6. Tools and Techniques

Code Formatting: Emphasize the importance of consistent code formatting to improve readability.

Documentation: Encourage the use of comments and documentation to explain the purpose and logic of the DSL code.

Refactoring: Discuss how refactoring techniques can be applied to DSL code to improve its structure and maintainability.

7. Measuring Readability

Code Metrics: Briefly mention code metrics that can be used to assess the readability of DSL code, such as code complexity and line length.

User Feedback: Emphasize the importance of gathering feedback from users to understand how readable and maintainable the DSL is in practice.

By highlighting the importance of readability and maintainability and demonstrating how DSLs can contribute to these qualities, we can show readers how DSLs can lead to more effective, understandable, and sustainable software development.

Chapter 9

Real-World Case Studies

9.1 Successful DSL Implementations

1. SQL (Structured Query Language)

Ubiquitous in Databases: Highlight how SQL has become the standard language for interacting with relational databases, used in countless applications across industries.

Declarative Power: Emphasize how SQL's declarative nature simplifies data retrieval and manipulation, making it accessible to a wide range of users.

Evolution and Standardization: Discuss the evolution of SQL standards and its widespread adoption by database vendors.

2. HTML (HyperText Markup Language) and CSS (Cascading Style Sheets)

Foundation of the Web: Explain how HTML and CSS are fundamental to the World Wide Web, enabling the creation of web pages and user interfaces.

Simplicity and Accessibility: Highlight their relatively simple syntax and how they have made web development accessible to a broad audience.

Continuous Evolution: Discuss the ongoing evolution of HTML and CSS standards to meet the demands of modern web development.

3. Domain-Specific Languages in DevOps

Ansible, Puppet, Chef: Show how these configuration management tools use DSLs to automate infrastructure provisioning and management.

Terraform: Explain how Terraform uses a DSL to define infrastructure as code, enabling consistent and reproducible deployments.

Kubernetes: Describe how Kubernetes uses a DSL to define and manage containerized applications, simplifying deployment and orchestration.

4. DSLs in Specific Industries

Finance: Mention examples of DSLs used in financial modeling, risk management, or algorithmic trading.

Healthcare: Discuss DSLs used for clinical decision support, medical imaging analysis, or healthcare data management.

Telecommunications: Highlight DSLs used for network configuration, service provisioning, or call routing.

5. Open-Source DSLs

ANTLR: Introduce ANTLR as a powerful parser generator that has been used to create numerous DSLs.

Xtext: Mention Xtext as a framework for building textual DSLs with IDE support.

Other Examples: Explore other open-source DSLs that have gained popularity in specific domains.

6. Analyzing Success Factors

Clear Domain Focus: Emphasize how successful DSLs are often focused on a specific domain, providing a tailored solution to a particular set of problems.

Usability: Highlight the importance of usability in DSL adoption, ensuring that the DSL is easy to learn and use.

Community Support: Discuss the role of community support in the success of open-source DSLs.

Tooling and Ecosystem: Explain how good tooling and a thriving ecosystem can contribute to the success of a DSL.

By showcasing these successful DSL implementations and analyzing the factors that contributed to their success, we can inspire readers to explore the potential of DSLs and create their own domain-specific solutions.

9.2 Lessons Learned and Best Practices

Sharing lessons learned and best practices is essential for helping others avoid common pitfalls and adopt effective strategies when creating and using DSLs. Here's what we can include in this section:

Lessons Learned

Start with a Clear Scope: Begin with a well-defined scope for your DSL, focusing on a specific problem or domain. Avoid trying to create a "one-size-fits-all" solution.

Prioritize Usability: Invest time in designing a DSL that is easy to learn, read, and use. Consider the target audience and their familiarity with language concepts.

Iterative Development: Develop the DSL iteratively, gathering feedback from users and refining the design based on their needs and experiences.

Don't Over-Engineer: Avoid creating overly complex or abstract DSLs. Strive for simplicity and clarity.

Balance Abstraction and Control: Find the right balance between abstraction and control. DSLs should hide complexity but also allow for flexibility when needed.

Document Thoroughly: Provide clear and comprehensive documentation for the DSL, including its syntax, semantics, and examples of usage.

Testing is Crucial: Thoroughly test the DSL implementation to ensure its correctness and reliability. Use a variety of testing techniques and cover different scenarios.

Best Practices

Domain Analysis: Conduct a thorough analysis of the domain to identify key concepts, relationships, and tasks that the DSL should address.

User-Centered Design: Involve users in the design process to ensure the DSL meets their needs and expectations.

Leverage Existing Tools: Utilize existing tools and frameworks for DSL development, such as parser generators, code generation libraries, and IDE extensions.

Versioning and Evolution: Plan for versioning and evolution of the DSL to accommodate future changes and ensure backward compatibility.

Community Building: If creating an open-source DSL, foster a community around it to encourage adoption, contributions, and feedback.

Continuous Learning: Stay up-to-date with the latest trends and best practices in DSL development and language engineering.

Examples and Case Studies

Share real-world examples of DSL successes and failures, highlighting the lessons learned.

Analyze case studies of DSL implementations in different domains, discussing the challenges faced and the solutions adopted.

Tips for Sharing Lessons Learned

Be Specific: Provide concrete examples and specific details to illustrate the lessons learned.

Be Honest: Share both successes and failures, acknowledging mistakes and challenges encountered.

Be Constructive: Frame lessons learned in a constructive way, offering suggestions for improvement and best practices to follow.

Use a Variety of Formats: Share lessons learned through blog posts, articles, presentations, or even dedicated sections in the book.

By sharing these lessons learned and best practices, we can help readers avoid common pitfalls, make informed decisions, and create DSLs that are truly effective and valuable for their intended purpose.

9.3 Analyzing DSL Design Choices

Analyzing DSL design choices is a crucial step in creating a successful DSL. It involves reflecting on the decisions made during the design process and evaluating their impact on the DSL's usability, effectiveness, and maintainability. Here's how we can guide readers through this analysis:

1. Review the Design Goals

Original Motivation: Revisit the original goals and motivations for creating the DSL. Did the design choices effectively address the identified problems and needs?

Target Audience: Consider the target audience and their expertise. Were the design choices appropriate for their skill level and domain knowledge?

Success Metrics: How will you measure the success of the DSL? Are there specific metrics or criteria that can be used to evaluate its effectiveness?

2. Analyze the Design Decisions

Syntax:

Was the syntax clear, concise, and easy to understand?

Did it align well with the domain's terminology and concepts?

Were there any ambiguities or inconsistencies in the syntax?

Semantics:

Were the semantics of the DSL well-defined and unambiguous?

Did they accurately reflect the domain's rules and constraints?

Was the DSL expressive enough to capture the desired logic and behavior?

Abstraction Level:

Was the level of abstraction appropriate for the domain and the target audience?

Did it effectively hide complexity while still providing sufficient control?

Implementation:

Was the DSL implemented efficiently and maintainably?

Were there any performance bottlenecks or limitations?

Was the implementation flexible enough to accommodate future changes and extensions?

3. Evaluate the Impact

Usability:

How easy was it for users to learn and use the DSL?

Did they encounter any difficulties or confusion?

Was the DSL effective in improving their productivity and reducing errors?

Maintainability:

How easy is it to maintain and evolve the DSL?

Can the DSL be easily extended or modified to accommodate new requirements?

Is the DSL code well-documented and understandable?

Adoption:

Has the DSL been adopted by the intended users?

Are there any barriers to adoption that need to be addressed?

Community Feedback:

If the DSL is open-source, what feedback has been received from the community?

Are there any suggestions for improvement or areas where the DSL could be enhanced?

4. Tools and Techniques

Usability Testing: Conduct usability testing sessions with users to observe their interactions with the DSL and gather feedback.

Code Reviews: Perform code reviews to assess the quality and maintainability of the DSL implementation.

Surveys and Interviews: Gather feedback from users through surveys or interviews to understand their experiences and identify areas for improvement.

Metrics and Analytics: Track metrics related to DSL usage, such as the number of users, frequency of use, and types of errors encountered.

5. Iterative Refinement

Continuous Improvement: Emphasize that DSL design is an iterative process. Use the analysis and feedback to continuously refine and improve the DSL.

Versioning: Introduce new versions of the DSL to incorporate improvements and address limitations, while maintaining backward compatibility where possible.

Documentation Updates: Keep the documentation up-to-date to reflect changes and improvements in the DSL.

Chapter 10

Emerging Trends and Technologies

10.1 Analyzing DSL Design Choices

1. DSLs for Defining AI Models

Simplifying Model Specification: Explain how DSLs can provide a higher-level abstraction for defining AI models, hiding the complexities of underlying frameworks and algorithms.

Domain-Specific AI: Discuss how DSLs can be used to create AI models that are tailored to specific domains, incorporating domain knowledge and constraints.

Examples:

TensorFlow DSL: Mention TensorFlow's Keras API as a DSL for defining neural networks.

Domain-Specific ML Languages: Explore examples of DSLs for specific machine learning tasks, such as natural language processing or image recognition.

2. DSLs for AI Pipelines

Orchestrating AI Workflows: Explain how DSLs can be used to define and orchestrate complex AI pipelines, including data preprocessing, model training, evaluation, and deployment.

Workflow Automation: Discuss how DSLs can automate the execution of AI workflows, reducing manual effort and improving reproducibility.

Examples:

Kubeflow: Mention Kubeflow as a platform that uses DSLs to define and manage machine learning workflows on Kubernetes.

MLflow: Discuss MLflow as a tool that uses DSLs to track experiments, manage models, and deploy AI applications.

3. DSLs for Explainable AI (XAI)

Making AI Transparent: Explain how DSLs can be used to express and explain the behavior of AI models, making them more transparent and understandable.

Enhancing Trust and Accountability: Discuss how DSLs can help build trust in AI systems by providing insights into their decision-making processes.

Examples:

Rule-based DSLs: Mention rule-based DSLs that can be used to express the logic of AI models in a human-readable format.

Visualization DSLs: Explore DSLs that can be used to visualize the internal workings of AI models.

4. AI-Powered DSLs

Intelligent Code Completion: Discuss how AI can be used to enhance DSLs with intelligent code completion, suggesting relevant code snippets and automating repetitive tasks.

Automated Code Generation: Explain how AI can be used to generate DSL code from natural language descriptions or higher-level specifications.

Error Detection and Correction: Discuss how AI can be used to detect and correct errors in DSL code, improving code quality and reducing debugging time.

5. Challenges and Future Directions

DSL Design for AI: Discuss the challenges of designing DSLs for AI, such as balancing expressiveness and usability, and addressing the dynamic nature of AI models.

Integration with AI Frameworks: Explore the integration of DSLs with existing AI frameworks and tools.

AI for DSL Development: Discuss the potential for AI to assist in the development and maintenance of DSLs, such as automating testing and generating documentation.

By exploring the synergy between DSLs and AI, we can show readers how these technologies can complement each other to create more powerful, accessible, and trustworthy AI solutions. This section can highlight the exciting possibilities at the forefront of software development and inspire readers to explore the future of DSLs in the age of AI.

10.2 Cloud-Based DSL Development

1. Benefits of Cloud-Based DSL Development

Accessibility and Collaboration: Cloud platforms provide a centralized and accessible environment for DSL development, enabling teams to collaborate seamlessly regardless of location.

Scalability and Resource Management: Cloud resources can be easily scaled to meet the demands of DSL development, providing on-demand access to computing power, storage, and other resources.

Integrated Tooling: Cloud platforms often offer integrated development environments (IDEs), version control systems, and other tools that streamline DSL development workflows.

Simplified Deployment: Cloud platforms simplify the deployment and distribution of DSLs, making them easily accessible to users.

Community Building: Cloud-based platforms can foster communities around DSLs, facilitating knowledge sharing, collaboration, and support.

2. Cloud-Based DSL Tools and Platforms

Cloud IDEs: Discuss cloud-based IDEs (e.g., AWS Cloud9, Google Cloud Shell Editor, GitHub Codespaces) that provide a complete development environment for DSL creation.

Language Workbenches: Explore cloud-based language workbenches (e.g., Eclipse Che) that offer specialized tools for DSL development, including editors, debuggers, and code generators.

Serverless Platforms: Discuss how serverless platforms (e.g., AWS Lambda, Google Cloud Functions) can be used to deploy and execute DSL-based applications.

Cloud-Based APIs: Explain how cloud providers offer APIs that can be leveraged to create DSLs for interacting with cloud services and resources.

3. DSLs for Cloud Infrastructure

Infrastructure as Code (IaC): Reiterate how DSLs are used in IaC tools (e.g., Terraform, AWS CloudFormation) to define and manage cloud infrastructure.

Cloud-Specific DSLs: Discuss DSLs specifically designed for interacting with cloud services, such as managing virtual machines, storage, or databases.

Examples:

AWS Cloud Development Kit (CDK): Mention AWS CDK as a tool that allows developers to define cloud infrastructure using familiar programming languages.

Google Cloud Deployment Manager: Discuss Google Cloud Deployment Manager as a tool for deploying and managing cloud resources using YAML-based configurations.

4. Challenges and Considerations

Security: Address the security considerations of developing and deploying DSLs in the cloud, including protecting sensitive data and ensuring secure access control.

Vendor Lock-in: Discuss the potential for vendor lock-in when using cloud-specific DSLs and tools.

Cost Management: Explain how to effectively manage the costs associated with cloud-based DSL development and deployment.

5. Future Directions

AI and Machine Learning: Discuss how cloud-based AI/ML services can be integrated with DSLs to enhance code generation, error detection, and other development tasks.

Serverless DSLs: Explore the potential for serverless computing to simplify the deployment and execution of DSL-based applications.

Low-Code/No-Code Platforms: Discuss how cloud-based low-code/no-code platforms can leverage DSLs to empower citizen developers and accelerate application development.

By exploring the advantages, tools, and challenges of cloud-based DSL development, we can equip readers with the knowledge to leverage the power of the cloud for creating and deploying DSLs effectively. This section can highlight the evolving landscape of DSL development and inspire readers to explore new possibilities in the cloud era.

10.3 The Future of Language Engineering

The future of language engineering is brimming with exciting possibilities! As technology continues to advance at a rapid pace, the way we design, implement, and interact with languages is evolving. Here are some key trends and areas to explore in this section:

1. AI-Driven Language Engineering

AI-Assisted Language Design: Discuss how AI can assist in the design of new languages, analyzing patterns, suggesting improvements, and even generating code.

Automated Code Generation: Explore how AI can generate code from natural language descriptions or higher-level specifications, making programming more accessible.

Intelligent Code Completion: Discuss how AI can enhance code editors with more sophisticated and context-aware code completion suggestions.

AI-Powered Debugging: Explore how AI can assist in debugging by identifying potential errors, suggesting fixes, and even automatically generating tests.

2. Rise of Domain-Specific Languages (DSLs)

Proliferation of DSLs: Predict a continued increase in the creation and use of DSLs across various domains, driven by the need for more specialized and efficient tools.

DSL Frameworks and Tooling: Discuss the development of more sophisticated frameworks and tools for creating, managing, and deploying DSLs.

DSLs for Emerging Technologies: Explore the role of DSLs in emerging technologies like blockchain, quantum computing, and the Internet of Things (IoT).

3. Language Engineering for Quantum Computing

Quantum Programming Languages: Discuss the development of new programming languages specifically designed for quantum computing, addressing the unique challenges and opportunities of this paradigm.

Quantum DSLs: Explore the potential for DSLs to simplify quantum programming and make it more accessible to developers.

Quantum Algorithm Design: Discuss how language engineering can contribute to the design and optimization of quantum algorithms.

4. Language Engineering for the Metaverse

Languages for Virtual Worlds: Explore the development of languages for creating and interacting with virtual worlds and immersive experiences.

DSLs for 3D Modeling and Simulation: Discuss the role of DSLs in simplifying 3D modeling, animation, and simulation.

Languages for Human-Computer Interaction: Explore new language paradigms for natural and intuitive interaction with virtual environments.

5. Formal Verification and Security

Increased Emphasis on Security: Highlight the growing importance of language design for security, ensuring that languages are robust against vulnerabilities and attacks.

Formal Verification Techniques: Discuss the use of formal verification techniques to prove the correctness and security of language implementations.

Secure DSLs: Explore the design of DSLs that are inherently secure and resistant to common security threats.

6. Ethical Considerations

Responsible Language Design: Discuss the ethical considerations of language design, including bias, fairness, and inclusivity.

Language for Social Good: Explore how language engineering can be used to address social challenges and promote positive change.

AI Ethics in Language: Discuss the ethical implications of AI-driven language engineering, ensuring that these technologies are used responsibly and ethically.

7. Looking Ahead

Continuous Evolution: Emphasize that language engineering is a constantly evolving field, driven by technological advancements and changing needs.

Interdisciplinary Collaboration: Highlight the importance of interdisciplinary collaboration between language engineers, computer scientists, domain experts, and other stakeholders.

Open Source and Community: Encourage open-source contributions and community involvement in the development of new languages and tools.

By exploring these future directions and challenges, we can provide readers with a glimpse into the exciting possibilities of language engineering and inspire them to contribute to the future of language design and implementation.

www.ingramcontent.com/pod-product-compliance
Lightning Source LLC
Chambersburg PA
CBHW070355230526
45471CB00006B/2583